FOUR LAST THINGS

Sir Thomas More,
Chancellor of England

Edited by: D.P. Curtin

Dalcassian
Publishing
Company
PHILADELPHIA, PA

Library of Congress Cataloging-in-Publication Data

Copyright © 2023 Dalcassian Publishing Co.
In association with St. Macartan Press

Part 1--The Remembrance of Death
A TREATISE (UNFINISHED)
UPON THESE WORDS OF HOLY SCRIPTURE
Memorare novissima, & in aeternum non peccabis "Remember the last things, & thou shalt never sin."—Ecclus. 7 .
Made about the year of our Lord 1522, by Sir Thomas More then knight, and one of the Privy Council
of King Henry VIII, and also Under-Treasurer of England.

If there were any question among men whether the words of holy Scripture or the doctrine of any secular author were of greater force and effect to the weal and profit of man's soul (though we should let pass so many short and weighty words spoken by the mouth of our Saviour Christ Himself, to Whose heavenly wisdom the wit of none earthly creature can be comparable) yet this only text written by the wise man in the seventh chapter of Ecclesiasticus is such that it containeth more fruitful advice and counsel to the forming and framing of man's manners in virtue and avoiding of sin, than many whole and great volumes of the best of old philosophers or any other that ever wrote in secular literature.

Long would it be to take the best of their words and compare it with these words of holy Writ. Let us consider the fruit and profit of this in itself: which thing, well advised and pondered, shall well declare that of none whole volume of secular literature shall arise so very fruitful doctrine. For what would a man give for a sure medicine that were of such strength that it should all his life keep him from sickness, namely **1** if he might by the avoiding of sickness be sure to continue his life one hundred years? So is it now that these words giveth us all a sure medicine (if we forsloth **2** not the receiving) by which we shall keep from sickness, not the body, which none health may long keep from death (for die we must in few years, live we never so long), but the soul, which here preserved from the sickness of sin, shall after this eternally live in joy and be preserved from the deadly life of everlasting pain.
The physician sendeth his bill to the apothecary, and therein writeth sometimes a costly receipt of many strange herbs and roots, fetched out of far countries, long-lain drugs, all the strength worn out, and some none such to be got. But this physician sendeth his bill to thyself, no strange thing therein, nothing costly to buy, nothing far to fetch, but to be gathered all times of the year in the garden of thine own soul.

Let us hear, then, what wholesome receipt this is. "Remember," saith this bill, "thy last things, and thou shalt never sin in this world." Here is first a short medicine containing only four herbs, common and well known, that is to wit, death, doom, pain, and joy.

This short medicine is of a marvellous force, able to keep us all our life from sin. The physician cannot give no one medicine to every man to keep him from sickness, but to divers men divers, by reason of the diversity of divers complexions. This medicine serveth every man. The physician doth but guess and conjecture that his receipt shall do good; but this medicine is undoubtedly sure.

How happeth it, then, thou wilt haply say, that so few be preserved from sin, if every man have so sure a medicine, so ready at hand? For folk fare commonly as he doth that goeth forth fasting among sick folk for sloth, rather than he will take a little treacle **3** before.

Thou wilt say, peradventure, that some part of this medicine is very bitter and painful to receive. Surely there can be nothing so bitter but wisdom would brook it for so great a profit? But yet this medicine, though thou make a sour face at it, is not so bitter as thou makest for. **4** For well thou wottest, he biddeth thee not take neither death, nor doom, nor pain, but only to remember them, and yet the joy of heaven therewith to temper them withal. Now if a man be so dainty stomached that going where contagion is he would grudge to take a little treacle, **5** yet were he very nicely wanton if he might not at the leastwise take a little vinegar and rose water in his handkercher.
Yet wot I well that many one will say that the bare remembrance of death alone, if a man consider it and advise it well, were able to bereave a man of all the pleasure of his life. How much more, then, should his life be painful and grievous if, to the remembrance and consideration of death, a man should add and set to, the deep imagination of the dreadful doom of God, and bitter pains of purgatory or hell, of which every one passeth and exceedeth many deaths. These are the sage saws of such as make this world their heaven, and their lust their God.

Now see the blindness of us worldly folk, how precisely we presume to shoot our foolish bolt, in those matters most in which we least can skill. **6** For I little doubt but that among four thousand taken out at adventure, we shall not find four score but they shall boldly affirm it for a thing too painful, busily to remember these four last things. And yet durst I lay a wager that of those four thousand ye shall not find fourteen that hath deeply thought on them four times in all their days.

If men would vouchsafe to put in proof and experience the operation and working of this medicine, the remembrance of these four last things, they should find therein, not the pleasure of their life lost, but so great a pleasure grow thereby that they never felt the like before nor would have supposed that ever they should have felt any such. For it is to be known that, like as we be made of two far divers and unlike substances, the body and the soul, so we be apt and able to receive two diverse and unlike pleasures, the one carnal and fleshly, the other ghostly and spiritual. And like as the soul excelleth the body, so doth the sweetness of spiritual pleasure far pass and excel the gross and filthy pleasure of all fleshly delight, which is of truth no very true pleasure, but a false counterfeit image of pleasure. And the cause why men be so mad thereon is only for ignorance and lack of knowledge of the other,—as those that lack insight of precious stones hold themselves as well content and satisfied with a beryl or crystal well counterfeited, as with a right natural diamond. But he that by good use and experience hath in his eye the right mark and very true lustre of the diamond, rejecteth anon and listeth not to look upon the counterfeit, be it never so well handled, never so craftily polished. And trust it well that, in likewise, if men would well accustom themselves in the taste of spiritual pleasure and of that sweet feeling that virtuous people have of the good hope of heaven, they should shortly set at naught, and at length abhor, the foul delight and filthy liking that riseth of sensual and fleshly pleasure, which is never so pleasantly spiced with delight and liking but that it bringeth therewith such a grudge and grief of conscience that it maketh the stomach wamble 7 and fare as it would vomit. And that notwithstanding, such is our blind custom that we persevere therein without care or cure of the better, as a sow content with draff, 8 dirt and mire careth neither for better meat nor better bed.

Think not that everything is pleasant that men for madness laugh at. For thou shalt in Bedlam see one laugh at the knocking of his own head against a post, and yet there is little pleasure therein. But ye think peradventure this example as mad as the mad man, and as little to the purpose. I am content ye so think. But what will ye say if ye see men that are taken and reputed wise laugh much more madly than he? Shall ye not see such laugh at their own craft, when they have, as they think, wilfully done their neighbour wrong? Now whoso seeth not that his laughter is more mad than the laughter of the mad man, I hold him madder than they both. For the mad man laughed when he had done himself but little hurt, by a knock of his head to the post. This other sage fool laugheth at the casting of his own soul into the fire of hell, for which he hath cause to weep all his life. And it cannot be but the grudge and fear thereof followeth his laughter, and secret sorrow marreth all such outward mirth. For the heart of a wicked wretch is like a stormy sea that cannot rest, 9 except a man be fallen down into the dungeon of wretchedness, and the door shut over his head. For when a sinner is once fallen down into the depth, he waxeth a desperate wretch and setteth all at naught, and he is in the worst kind of all, and farthest from all recovery. For like as in the body his sickness is most incurable that is sick and feeleth it not, but weeneth himself whole (for he that is in that case is commonly mad), so he that by a mischievous custom of sin perceiveth no fault in his evil deed nor hath no remorse thereof, hath lost the natural light of reason and the spiritual light of faith, which two lights of knowledge and understanding quenched, what remaineth in him more than the bodily senses and sensual wits common to man and brute beasts?

Now albeit so that the fleshly and worldly pleasure is of truth not pleasant but bitter, and the spiritual pleasure is of truth so sweet that the sweetness thereof many times darkeneth **10** and diminisheth the feeling of bodily pain, by reason whereof good virtuous folk feel more pleasure in the sorrow of their sins and affliction of their penance than wretches feel in the fulfilling of their foul delight, and credible is it that the inward spiritual pleasure and comfort which many of the old holy martyrs had in the hope of heaven darkened **11** and in manner overwhelmed the bodily pains of their torment,—yet this notwithstanding, like as a sick man feeleth no sweetness in sugar, and some women with child have such fond lust that they had liefer eat tar than treacle and rather pitch than marmalade, and some whole people love tallow better than butter, and Iceland loveth no butter till it be long barrelled, so we gross carnal people, having our taste infected by the sickness of sin and filthy custom of fleshly lust, find so great liking in the vile and stinking delectation of fleshly delight that we list not once prove what manner of sweetness good and virtuous folk feel and perceive in spiritual pleasure. And the cause is why? Because we cannot perceive the one, but if we forbear the other. For like as the ground that is all forgrown **12** with nettles, briars, and other evil weeds, can bring forth no corn till they be weeded out, so can our soul have no place for the good corn of spiritual pleasure as long as it is overgrown with the barren weeds of carnal delectation. For the pulling out of which weeds by the root, there is not a more meet instrument than of the remembrance of the four last things, which as they shall pull out these weeds of fleshly voluptuousness, so shall they not fail to plant in their places, not only wholesome virtues, but also marvellous ghostly pleasure and spiritual gladness, which in every good soul riseth of the love of God, and hope of heaven, and inward liking that the godly spirit taketh in the diligent labour of good and virtuous business.

I would not so long tarry in this point nor make so many words of the pleasure that men may find by the receipt of this medicine, were it not that I well perceive the world so set upon the seeking of pleasure, that they set by pleasure much more than by profit. And therefore, to the intent that ye may perceive that it is not a fantasy found **13** of mine own head, that the abandoning and refusing of carnal pleasure and the ensuing of labour, travail, penance and bodily pain, shall bring therewith to a Christian man, not only in the world that is coming but also in this present life, very sweetness, comfort, pleasure, and gladness, I shall prove it to be true by their testimony and witness whose authority, speaking of their own experience, there will, I ween, none honest man mistrust.

Lo, the holy doctor, Saint Austin, exhorting penitents and repentant sinners to sorrow for their offences, saith unto them: "Sorrow," saith this holy man, "and be glad of thy sorrow." In vain should he bid him be glad of his sorrow, if man in sorrow could not be glad. But this holy father showeth by this counsel, not only that a man may be joyful and glad for all his sorrow, but also that he may be and hath cause to be glad because of his sorrow.
Long were it to rehearse the places that prove this point among the holy doctors of Christ's Church; but we will, instead of them all, allege you the words of Him that is doctor of them all, our Saviour Jesu Christ. He saith that the way to heaven is strait and aspre **14** or painful. **15** And therefore He saith that few folk find it out or walk therein. And yet saith He for all that, "My yoke is easy and my burden light." **16** How could these two sayings stand together, were it not that as the labour, travail, and affliction of the body is painful and sharp to the flesh, so the comfort and gladness that the soul conceiveth thereof, rising into the love of our Lord and hope of His glory to come, so tempereth and overmastereth the bitterness of the grief, that it maketh the very labour easy, the sourness very sweet, and the very pain pleasant?

Will ye see the example? Look upon His holy apostles,—when they were taken and scourged with whips for Christ's sake, did it grieve them, think ye? Imagine yourself in the same case, and I think ye will think yea. Now see, then, for all the pain of their flesh, what joy and pleasure they conceived in their soul. The holy Scripture saith **17** that they rejoiced and joyed that God had accounted them worthy for Christ's sake, not only to be scourged, but also—which would be far greater grief to an honest man than the pain itself—to be scourged with despite and shame, so that the more their pain was, the more was their joy. For as the holy doctor, Saint Chrysostom, saith, though pain be grievous for the nature of the affliction, yet is it pleasant by the alacrity and quick mind of them that willingly suffer it. And therefore, though the nature of the torments make great grief and pain, yet the prompt and willing mind of them that were scourged passed and overcame the nature of the thing, that is to wit, mastering the outward fleshly pain with inward spiritual pleasure. And surely this is so true that it may stand for a very certain token that a penitent beginneth to profit and grow in grace and favour of God when he feeleth a pleasure and quickness in his labour and pain taken in prayer, almsdeeds, pilgrimage, fasting, discipline, tribulation, affliction, and such other spiritual exercise, by which the soul willingly worketh with the body by their own punishment to purge and rub out the rusty, cankered spots that sin hath defiled them with in the sight of God, and to leave the fewer to be burned out in the fire of purgatory. And whensoever, as I say, that a man feeleth in this pain a pleasure he hath a token of great grace and that his penance is pleasant to God, for, as the holy Scripture saith, our Lord loveth a glad giver. **18** And on the other side, whereas one doth such spiritual business with a dulness of spirit and weariness of mind, he doth twice as much and thereby taketh four times as much pain, since his bodily pain is relieved with no spiritual rejoice nor comfort. I will not say that his labour is lost, but I dare be bold to say that he profiteth much less with much more pain. For certain it is that the best souls and they that have best travailed in spiritual business, find most comfort therein. **19** And therefore if they most pleased God that in the bodily pain of their penance took less spiritual pleasure, it should thereof follow that the farther a man proceeded in the perfection of spiritual exercise, in the worse case he were. Which can in no wise be so, since that we see the holy apostles and other holy men and women, the better that they were, the more pleasure they perceived in their fleshly afflictions, either put unto them by God, or taken by themselves for God's sake.

Therefore let every man by the labour of his mind and help of prayer, enforce himself in all tribulation and affliction, labour, pain and travail, without spot of pride or ascribing any praise to himself, to conceive a delight and pleasure in such spiritual exercise, and thereby to rise in the love of our Lord, with an hope of heaven, contempt of the world, and longing to be with God. To the attaining of which mind, by the putting away of the malicious pleasures of the devil, the filthy pleasures of the flesh, and the vain pleasures of the world, which once excluded there is place made and clean purged to receive the very sweet and pure pleasure of the spirit,—there is not any one thing lightly, as I have said, more accommodated nor more effectual than this thing that I have begun with and taken in hand to entreat, that is to wit, the remembrance of the four last things, which is, as the Scripture saith, so effectual that if a man remember it well, he shall never sin.

Thou wilt haply say that it is not enough that a man do none evil, but he must also do good. This is very truth that ye say. But first, if there be but these two steps to heaven, he that getteth him on the one is half up. And over that, whoso doth none evil, it will be very hard but he must needs do good, since man's mind is never idle but occupied commonly either with good or evil. And therefore, when folk have few words and use much musing, likewise as among many words all be not always well and wisely set, so, when the tongue lieth still, if the mind be not occupied well it were less evil, save for worldly rebuke, to blabber on trifles somewhat sottishly, than while they seem sage in keeping silence, secretly peradventure the meanwhile to fantasy with

themselves filthy sinful devices, whereof their tongues, if they were set on babbling, could not for shame utter and speak the like.
I say not this for that I would have folks fall to babbling, well wotting that, as the Scripture saith, in many words lacketh not sin **20** —but that I would have folk in their silence take good heed that their minds be occupied with good thoughts, for unoccupied be they never. For if ever the mind
were empty, it would be empty when the body sleepeth. But if it were then all empty, we should have no dreams. Then, if the fantasies leave us not sleeping, it is not likely that ever they leave us waking. Wherefore, as I say, let us keep our minds occupied with good thoughts, or else the devil will fill them with evil.

And surely everything hath his mean. There is, as Scripture saith, time to speak and time to keep thy tongue. **21** Whensoever the communication is naught **22** and ungodly, it is better to hold thy tongue and think on some better thing the while, than to give ear thereto and underpin **23** the tale. And yet better were it than holding of thy tongue, properly to speak, and with some good grace and pleasant fashion to break into some better matter; by which thy speech and talking, thou shalt not only profit thyself as thou shouldst have done by thy well minded silence, but also amend the whole audience, which is a thing far better and of much more merit. Howbeit, if thou can find no proper means to break the tale, then, except thy bare authority suffice to command silence, it were peradventure good, rather to keep a good silence thyself, than blunder forth rudely and irritate them to anger, which shall haply therefor not let **24** to talk on, but speak much the more, lest they should seem to leave at thy commandment. And better were it for the while to let one wanton word pass uncontrolled, than give occasion of twain. But if the communication be good, then is it better not only to give ear thereto, but also first well and prudently to devise with thyself upon the same, and then moderately and in good manner, if thou find aught to the purpose, speak thereto and say thy mind therein. So shall it appear to the presence, **25** that your mind was well occupied the while and your thought not wandering forty miles thence while your body was there; as it often happeth that the very face showeth the mind walking a pilgrimage, in such wise that, not without some note and reproach of such vagrant mind, other folk suddenly say to them: 'A penny for your thoughts.' Which manner of wandering mind in company may percase be the more excusable sometimes by some chargeable business of the party, but surely it is never taken for wisdom nor good manners.

But now to return to my purpose, since the remembrance of these four last things is of such force and efficacy that it is able always to keep us from sin, and since we can never be long void of both, it must thereof ensue that we shall consequently do good; and thereof must it needs follow that this only lesson well learned and busily put in ure **26** must needs lead us to heaven. Yet will ye peradventure say that ye know these four things well enough, and if the knowledge thereof had so great effect as the Scripture speaketh of, there should not be so many naught **27** as there be. For what Christian man is he, that hath wit and discretion, but he hath heard and, having any faith, believeth these four last things, of which the first, that is to say, death, we need no faith to believe, we know it by daily proof and experience? I say not nay, but that we know them either by faith or experience,—and yet not so very thoroughly as we might, peradventure, and hereafter undoubtedly shall. Which if we knew once thoroughly, and so feelingly perceived as we might, percase, and namely as we surely shall, there would be little doubt but the least of all the four would well keep us from sin. For as for yet, though we have heard of the doom, yet were we never at it: though we have heard of hell, yet came we never in it; though we have heard of heaven, yet came we never to it; and though we daily see men die, and thereby know the death, yet ourselves never felt it. For if we knew these things thoroughly, the least of all four were, as I said, enough to keep us from sin.

Howbeit, the foresaid words of Scripture biddeth thee not know the four last things, but remember thy four last things, and then, he saith, thou shall never sin.

Many things know we that we seldom think on: and in the things of the soul, the knowledge without the remembrance little profiteth. What availeth it to know that there is a God, which thou not only believest by faith but also knowest by reason, what availeth that thou knowest Him, if thou think little of Him? The busy minding of thy four last things, and the deep consideration thereof, is the thing that shall keep thee from sin. And if thou put it in essay and make a proof, thou shalt well find, by that thou shalt have no lust to sin for the time that thou deeply thinkest on them, that if our frailty could endure never to remit or slacken in the deep devising of them, we should never have delight or pleasure in any sinful thing.

For the proof whereof, let us first begin at the remembrance of the first of these four last, which is undoubtedly far the least of the four, and thereby shall we make a proof what marvellous effect may grow by the diligent remembrance of all four, towards the avoiding of all the trains, **28** darts, sleights, enticings, and assaults of the three mortal enemies, the devil, the world, and our own flesh.

The Remembrance of Death. What profit and commodity cometh unto man's soul by the meditation of death is not only marked of **29** the chosen people of

God, but also of such as were the best sort among gentiles and paynims. For some of the old famous philosophers, when they were demanded what faculty philosophy was, answered that it was the meditation or exercise of death. For like as death maketh a severance of the body and the soul, when they by course of nature must needs depart asunder, so (said they) doth the study of philosophy labour to sever the soul from the love and affections of the body while they be together. Now if this be the whole study and labour of philosophy, as the best philosophers said that it is, then may we within short time be well learned in philosophy. For nothing is there that may more effectually withdraw the soul from the wretched affections of the body than may the remembrance of death,—if we do not remember it hoverly, **30** as one heareth a word and let it pass by his ear, without any receiving of the sentence **31** into his heart. But if we not only hear this word 'death,' but also let sink into our hearts the very fantasy and deep imagination thereof, we shall perceive thereby that we were never so greatly moved by the beholding of the Dance of Death pictured in Paul's, as we shall feel ourselves stirred and altered by the feeling of that imagination in our hearts. And no marvel. For those pictures express only the loathly figure of our dead bony bodies, bitten away the flesh; which though it be ugly to behold, yet neither the light thereof, nor the sight of all the dead heads in the charnel house, nor the apparation of a very ghost, is half so grisly as the deep conceived fantasy of death in his nature, by the lively imagination graven in thine own heart. For there seest thou, not one plain grievous sight of the bare bones hanging by the sinews, but thou seest (if thou fantasy thine own death, for so art thou by this counsel advised), thou seest, I say, thyself, if thou die no worse death, yet at the leastwise lying in thy bed, thy head shooting, thy back aching, thy veins beating, thine heart panting, thy throat rattling, thy flesh trembling, thy mouth gaping, thy nose sharping, thy legs cooling, thy fingers fumbling, thy breath shortening, all thy strength fainting, thy life vanishing, and thy death drawing on.

If thou couldst now call to thy remembrance some of those sicknesses that have most grieved thee and tormented thee in thy days, as every man hath felt some, and then findest thou that some one disease in some one part of thy body, as percase the stone or the strangury, have put thee to thine own mind to no less torment than thou shouldst have felt if one had put up a knife into the same place, and wouldst, as thee then seemed, have been content with such a change,—think what it will be then when thou shalt feel so many such pains in every part of thy body, breaking thy veins and thy life strings, with like pain and grief as though as many knives as thy body might receive should everywhere enter and meet in the midst. A stroke of a staff, a cut of a knife, the flesh singed with fire, the pain of sundry sickness, many men have essayed in themselves; and they that have not yet, somewhat have heard by them that felt it. But what manner dolour and pain, what manner of grievous pangs, what intolerable torment, the silly creature feeleth in the dissolution and severance of the soul from the body, never was there body that yet could tell the tale.

Some conjecture and token of this point we have of the bitter passion and piteous departing of our Saviour Jesu Christ, of Whom we nothing read that ever He cried for any pain, neither for the whips and rods beating His blessed body nor the sharp thorns pricking His holy head, or the great, long nails piercing His precious hands and feet. But when the point approached in which His sacred soul should depart out of His blessed body, at that point He cried loud once or twice to His Father in heaven, into Whose mighty and merciful hands, at the extreme point, with a great loud cry He gave up the ghost. **32** Now if that death was so painful and ragious to our Saviour Christ, Whose joy and comfort of His godhead, if He would have suffered it, might in such wise have redounded into His soul, and so forth into His body, that it should not only have supped up all His pain, but also have transformed His holy body into a glorious form and made it impossible,— what intolerable torment will death be then to us miserable wretches, of which the more part among the pangs of our passage shall have yet so painful twitches of our own conscience that the fear of hell, the dread of the devil, and sorrow at our heart at the sight of our sins, shall pass and exceed the deadly pains of our body. Other things are there which will peradventure seem no great matter to them that feel them not, but unto him that shall lie in that case, they shall be tedious out of all measure.

Have ye not ere this, in a sore sickness, felt it very grievous to have folk babble to you, and namely **33** such things as ye should make answer to, when it was a pain to speak? Think ye not now that it will be a gentle pleasure, when we lie dying, all our body in pain, all our mind in trouble, our soul in sorrow, our heart all in dread while our life walketh awayward, while our death draweth toward, while the devil is busy about us, while we lack stomach and strength to bear any one of so manifold heinous troubles, will it not be, as I was about to say, a pleasant thing to see before thine eyes and hear at thine ear a rabble of fleshly friends, or rather of flesh flies, skipping about thy bed and thy sick body, like ravens about thy corpse, now almost carrion, crying to thee on every side, "What shall I have? What shall I have?" Then shall come thy children and cry for their parts; then shall come thy sweet wife, and where in thine health haply she spake thee not one sweet word in six weeks, now shall she call thee sweet husband and weep with much work and ask thee what shall she have; then shall thine executors ask for the keys, and ask what money is owing thee, ask what substance thou hast, and ask where thy money lieth. And while thou liest in that case, their words shall be so tedious that thou wilt wish all that they ask for upon a red fire, so thou mightest lie one half-hour in rest.

Now is there one thing which a little I touched before, I wot not whether more painful or more perilous,—the marvellous intent business and solicitation of our ghostly enemy the devil, not only in one fashion present, but surely never absent from him that draweth towards death. For since that of his pestilent envy conceived from the beginning of man's creation, by which he lay in wait to take our first mother, Eve, in a train, and thereby drawing our former father, Adam, into the breach of God's behest, found the means not without the grievous increase of his own damnation, to deprive us of paradise and bereave us our immortality, making us into subjection not only of temporal death but also of his eternal tormentry, were we not by the great bounty of God and Christ's painful passion, restored to the possibility of everlasting life, he never ceased since to run about like a ramping lion, **34** looking whom he might devour,—it can be no doubt but he most busily travaileth in that behalf at the time that he perceiveth us about to depart hence.

For well he knoweth that then he either winneth a man for ever, or for ever loseth him; for have he him never so fast afore, yet if he break from him then he can after his death never get him again. Well he may, peradventure, have him as his gaoler in his prison of purgatory for the time of his punition temporal; but as he would have him for his perpetual slave, shall he never have him after, how sure soever he had him afore, if he get from him at the time of his death. For so lost he suddenly the thief that hung on the right hand of Christ. And on the other side, if he catch a man fast at the time of his death, he is sure to keep him for ever. For as the Scripture saith, "Wheresoever the stone **35** falleth, there shall it abide." **36** And since he knoweth this for very surety and is of malice so venomous and envious that he had liefer double his own pain than suffer us to escape from pain, he, when we draw to death, doth his uttermost endeavour to bring us to damnation, never ceasing to minister, by subtle and incogitable **37** means, first unlawful longing to live and horror to go gladly to God at His calling. Then giveth he some false glade **38** of escaping that sickness, and thereby putteth in our mind a love yet and cleaving to the world, keeping of our goods, loathsomeness of shrift, sloth towards good works. And if we be so far gone that we see we cannot recover, then he casteth in our minds presumption and security of salvation as a thing well won by our own works, of which, if we have any done well, he casteth them into our minds with over great liking and thereby withdraweth us from the haste of doing any more, as a thing that either needeth not or may be done by our executors. And instead of sorrow for our sins and care of heaven, he putteth us in mind of provision for some honourable burying,—so many torches, so many tapers, so many black gowns, so many merry mourners laughing under black hoods, and a gay hearse, with the delight of goodly and honourable funerals: in which the foolish sick man is sometimes occupied as though he thought that he should stand in a window and see how worshipfully he shall be brought to church. And thus inveigleth he them that either be good, or but meetly **39** bad.

But as for those that he hath known for special wretches, whose whole life hath in effect been all bestowed in his service, whom he hath brought into great and horrible sins by the horror whereof he hath kept them from confession, these folk at their end he handleth on another fashion. For into their minds he bringeth their shameful sins by heap, and by the abominable sight thereof draweth them into desperation. For the aggrieving whereof our Lord, after their deserving, suffereth him to show himself to them for their more discomfort in some fearful figure and terrible likeness, by the beholding whereof they conceive sometimes despair of salvation and yield themselves as captives quick, beginning their hell in this world, as hath appeared by the words and wretched behaviour of many that of a shameful, sinful life have died and departed with heavy desperate death. Now death being such as I have described, or rather much more horrible than any man can describe, it is not to be doubted but if we busily remembered the terror and grief thereof, it must needs be so bitter to the fleshly mind that it could not fail to take away the vain delight of all worldly vanities. But the thing that letteth **40** us to consider death in his kind, and to take great profit that would arise of the remembrance thereof is that for by the hope of long life, we look upon death either so far off that we see him not at all, or but a slight and uncertain sight, as a man may see a thing so far off that he wotteth not whether it be a bush or a beast. And surely so fare we by death, looking thereat afar off through a great long space of as many years as we hope to live,—and those we imagine many, and perilously and foolishly beguile ourselves. For likewise as wives would their husbands should ween by the example of Sarah that there were no woman so old but she might have a child, so is there none old man so old but that, as Tully **41** saith, he trusteth to live one year yet. And as for young folk, they look not how many be dead in their own days younger than themselves, but who is the oldest man in the town, and upon his years they make their reckoning,—where the wiser way were to reckon that a young man may die soon, and an old man cannot live long, but within a little while die the one may, the other must. And with this reckoning shall they look upon death much nearer hand, and better perceive him in his own likeness, and thereby take the more fruit of the remembrance and make themselves the more ready thereto.

Thou wouldst somewhat remember death the more effectually, and look upon him somewhat the more nearly, if thou knewest thyself sick, and specially of any perilous sickness that would make an end of thee though thou feltest yet little pain. For commonly when we be sick then begin we to know ourselves, then pain bringeth us home, **42** then we think how merry a thing it were to be praying in health, which we cannot now do for grief. Then care we little for our gay gear, then desire we no delicate dainties; and as for Lady Lechery, then abhor we to think on. And then we think in ourselves that if ever we recover and mend in body, we will amend in soul, leave all vices and be virtuously occupied the remnant of our life. Insomuch that very true we find the words of the epistle that the well-learned man, Plinius Secundus, after his sickness wrote unto his friend, wherein, after the description of men's fantasies in their disease, he closeth up his letter in this wise: "Look," saith he, "all the good counsel and precepts that all the philosophers and wise men in this world give us for instruction of virtuous living, all that can I compendiously give to myself and thee in few words: no more, lo, but let us be such when we be whole, as we think we will be when we be sick."

Now then if thou be ever sick, and ever sick of a perilous sickness, wouldst thou not, if thou knewest thyself in such case, have better remembrance of death than thou hast? It would be hard, peradventure, to make thee believe thyself sick while thou feelest no harm, and yet is that no sure knowledge of health. Trow ye not that many a man is infected with the great sickness a good while ere he perceive it, and the body sore corrupt within ere he feel the grief? How many men have there been that have gone about with God's marks on their body, never perceiving themselves to be sick, but as merry as ever they were in their lives, till other men gave them warning how near they were their deaths? And therefore never reckon thyself whole, though thou feel no grief.

But thou wilt haply say, "Be it that I cannot surely reckon myself whole, yet ye show me not why I should reckon myself sick." Thou sayest right well, and that shall I show thee now. Tell me, if one were in case that he must be fain once or twice a day to swaddle and plaster his leg and else he could not keep his life, wouldst thou reckon his leg sick or whole? I ween ye will agree that his leg is not well at ease, nor the owner neither. Now if ye felt your belly in such case that ye must be fain all day to tend it with warm clothes **43** or else ye were not able to abide the pain, would ye reckon your belly sick or whole? I ween ye would reckon your belly not in good quart. **44** If thou shouldst see one in such case that he could not hold up his head, that he could not stand on his feet, that he should be fain to lie down along and there lie speechless as a dead stock an hour or two every day, wouldst thou not say that he were perilously sick and had good cause to remember death, when he lieth every day in such case as though he were dead already?

Now then I pray thee consider me that all our bodies be ever in such case so tender of themselves that except we lapped them continually with warm clothes, we were not able to live one winter week. Consider that our bodies have so sore a sickness and such a continual consumption in themselves that the strongest were not able to endure and continue ten days together, were it not that once or twice a day we be fain to take medicines inward to clout them up withal and keep them as long as we can. For what is our meat and drink but medicines against hunger and thirst, that give us warning of that we daily lose by our inward consumption? And of that consumption shall we die in conclusion, for all the medicines that we use, though never other sickness came at us.

Consider also that all our swaddling and tending with warm clothes and daily medicines, yet can our bodies not bear themselves but that almost half our time ever in twenty-four hours we be fain to fall in a swoon which we call sleep, and there lie like dead stocks by a long space ere we come to ourselves again: insomuch that among all wise men of old it is agreed that sleep is the very image of death.

Now thou wilt peradventure say that this is but a fantasy. For though we call this hunger sickness and meat a medicine, yet men know well enough what very **45** sickness is and what very medicines be, and thereby we know well enough that they be none.

If thou think this, then would I wit of thee what thou callest a sickness. Is not that a sickness that will make an end of thee if it be not helped? If that be so, then I suppose thou bearest ever thy sickness with thee,—for very sure art thou that it will make an end of thee if thou be not helped.

What callest thou, then, a medicine? Is it not such a thing as either applied outwardly to thy body, or received inward, shall preserve thee against that sore or sickness that else would put thee or some part of thee in peril? What can be, then, more properly and more verily a medicine than is our meat and drink, by which is resisted the peril and undoubted death that else should in so few days follow, by the inward sickness of our own nature continually consuming us within? For as for that ye reckon that we know which be sickness, that is but a custom of calling, by which we call no sickness by that name but such as be casual and come and go. For that that is common to all men, and never from any man, because we reckon it natural, we give it not the name of sickness, but we name sickness a passion **46** that cometh seldomer and, as we reckon, against nature, whereas the conflict of the divers qualified elements tempered in our body, continually labouring each to vanquish other and thereby to dissolve the whole, though it be as sore against the continuance of our nature and as sore laboureth to the dissolution of the whole body as other sickness do, yet we neither call it sickness, nor the meat that resisteth it we call no medicine, and that for none other cause but for the continual familiarity that we have therewith.

But now consider, if it were so that one whole country were born all lepers, which is a sickness rather foul and perilous than painful, or all an whole country born with the falling sickness, so that never any of them had ever in their lives known or heard either themselves or any other void of those diseases, trow ye this, then, that they would ever have reckoned them for sickness? Nay surely, but they would have counted for sickness the colic and the stone and such other like as come and go. But as for their leprosy and falling evil, they would never account it other than we account hunger or sleep. For as for that thy hunger doth thee pleasure when it is fed, so doth sometimes the itch of a sore leg when thou clawest about the brinks. **47** And thus mayest thou surely see that all our whole life is but a sickness never curable, but as an incurable canker, with continual swaddling and plastering botched up to live as long as we may, and in conclusion undoubtedly to die of the same sickness, and though there never came other. So that, if you consider this well, thou mayest look upon death, not as a stranger, but as a nigh neighbour. For as the flame is next the smoke, so is death next an incurable sickness; and such is all our life.

And yet if this move you little, but that ye think for all this that death is far from you, I will go somewhat nearer you. Thou reckonest every man near his death when he is dying. Then if thyself be now already dying, how canst thou reckon thyself far from death? Some man saith merrily to his fellow, "Be merry, man,—thou shalt never die as long as thou livest." And albeit he seem to say true, yet saith he more than he can make good. For if that were true, I could make him much merrier, for then he should never die. Ye will peradventure marvel of this, but it is easy to prove. For I think ye will grant me that there is no time after that a man hath once life, but he is either alive or dead. Then will there no man say that one can die either before he get life or after that he hath lost it, and so hath he no time left to die in but while he hath life. Wherefore, if we neither die before our life nor when we be dead already, needs must it follow that we never die but while we live.
It is not all one to die and to be dead. Truth it is that we be never dead while we live; and it is, meseemeth, as true, not only that we die while we live, but also that we die all the while we live. What thing is dying? Is it any other thing than the passage and going out of this present life?

Now tell me, then, if thou were going out of an house, whether art thou going out only when thy foot is on the uttermost inch of the threshold, thy body half out of the door, or else when thou beginnest to set the first foot forward to go out, in what place of the house soever ye stand when ye buskle **48** forward? I would say that ye be going out of the house from the first foot ye set forward to go forth. No man will think other, as I suppose, but all is one reason in going hence and coming hither. Now if one were coming hither to this town, he were not only coming hither while he were entering in at the gate, but all the way also from whence he came hitherward. Nor, in likewise, in going hence from this town,—a man is not only going from this town while he hath his body in the gate going outward, but also while he setteth his foot out of his host's house to go forward. And therefore, if a man met him by the way, far yet within the town, and asked him whither he were going, he should truly answer that he were going out of the town, all were the town so long that he had ten miles to go ere he came at the gate.

And surely, methinketh that in likewise a man is not only dying, that is to say, going in his way out of this life, while he lieth drawing on, but also all the while that he is going towards his end,—which is by all the whole time of his life, since the first moment till the last finished, that is to wit, since the first moment in which he began to live, until the last moment of his life, or rather the first in which he is fully dead.

Now if this be thus, as meseemeth that reason proveth, a man is always dying from afore his birth, and every hour of our age, as it passeth by, cutteth his own length out of our life and maketh it shorter by so much, and our death so much the nearer. Which measuring of time and diminishing of life, with approaching towards death, is nothing else but from our beginning to our ending, one continual dying: so that wake we, sleep we, eat we, drink we, mourn we, sing we, in what wise soever live we, all the same while die we. So that we never ought to look towards death as a thing far off, considering that although he made no haste towards us, yet we never cease ourselves to make haste towards him.

Now if thou think this reason but a sophistical subtlety, and thinkest while thou art a young man thou mayest for all this think thy death far off, that is to wit, as far as thou hast by likelihood of nature many years to live, then will I put thee an homely example, not very pleasant, but none the less very true and very fit for the matter.

If there were two, both condemned to death, both carried out at once towards execution; of which two, the one were sure that the place of his execution were within one mile, the other twenty miles off, yea an hundred, an ye will, he that were in the cart to be carried an hundred miles would not take much more pleasure than his fellow in the length of his way, notwithstanding that it were a hundred times as long as his fellow's and that he had thereby a hundred times as long to live, being sure and out of all question to die at the end.

Reckon me now yourself a young man in your best lust, twenty years of age, if ye will. Let there be another, ninety. Both must ye die, both be ye in the cart carrying forward. His gallows and death standeth within ten miles at the farthest, and yours within eighty. I see not why ye should reckon much less of your death than he, though your way be longer, since ye be sure ye shall never cease riding till ye come at it. And this is true, although ye were sure that the place of your execution stood so far beyond his. But what if there were to the place of your execution two ways, of which the one were four score miles farther about than your fellow's, the other nearer by five miles than his; and when ye were put in the cart, had warning of both; and though ye were showed that it were likely that ye should be carried the longer way, yet it might hap ye should go the shorter, and whether ye were carried the one or the other, ye should never know till ye come to the place: I trow ye could not in this case make much longer of your life than of your fellow's.

Now in this case are we all. For our Lord hath not indented **49** with us of the time. **50** He hath appointed what we may not pass, but not how soon we shall go, nor where, nor in what wise. And therefore if thou wilt consider how little cause thou hast to reckon thy death so far off by reason of thy youth, reckon how many as young as thou have been slain in the selfsame ways in which thou ridest, how many have been drowned in the selfsame waters in which thou rowest. And thus shalt thou well see that thou hast no cause to look upon thy death as a thing far off, but a thing undoubtedly nigh thee, and ever walking with thee. By which, not a false imagination but a very true contemplation, thou shalt behold him and advise **51** him such as he is, and thereby take occasion to flee vain pleasures of the flesh that keep out the very **52** pleasures of the soul.

1 especially.
2 postpone.
3 a prophylactic.
4 pretend.
5 a prophylactic.
6 have least knowledge.
7 uneasy.
8 refuse, hogwash.
9 Is. lvii. 20.
10 deadens.
11 deadens.
12 overgrown.
13 contrived, invented.

14 *sharp.*
15 *Matt. vii. 14.*
16 *Matt. xi. 30.*
17 *Acts. v. 41.*
18 *2 Cor. ix. 7.*
19 *Cf. Dialogue Concerning Tyndale, p. 151.*
20 *Prov. x. 19.*
21 *Eccles. iii. 7.*
22 *the talk is evil.*
23 *support.*
24 *refrain.*
25 *those present.*
26 *into practice.*
27 *evil.*
28 *schemes, plots.*
29 *observed in.*
30 *inattentively.*
31 *meaning.*
32 *Matt. xxvii. 50; Mark xv. 37; Luke xxiii. 46.*
33 *especially.*
34 *Ps. xxi. 14; 1 Pet. v. 8.*
35 *rather, tree.*
36 *Eccles. xi. 3.*
37 *incalculable.*
38 *opening.*
39 *moderately.*
40 *prevents.*
41 *Cicero.*
42 *brings things home to us.*
43 *hot compresses.*
44 *health, condition.*
45 *real.*
46 *suffering.*
47 *edges.*
48 *start.*
49 *entered into an agreement.*
50 *Job xiv. 13.*
51 *mark, heed, consider.*
52 *true.*

Part 2--Of Pride and Envy

Of Pride. Now since I have somewhat laid afore thy face the bodily pains of death, the troubles and vexations spiritual that come therewith by thy ghostly enemy the devil, the unrestful cumbrance of thy fleshly friends, the uncertainty of thyself, how soon this dreadful time shall come, that thou art ever sick of that incurable sickness by which, if none other come, thou shalt yet in few years undoubtedly die, and yet, moreover, that thou art already dying, and ever hast been since thou first beganst to live,—let us now make some proof of this one part of our medicine, how the remembrance of death, in this fashion considered in his kind, will work with us to the preservation of our souls from every kind of sin, beginning at the sin that is the very head and root of all sins, that is to wit, pride, the mischievous mother of all manner vice.

I have seen many vices ere this that at the first seemed far from pride, and yet well considered to the uttermost it would well appear that of that root they sprang. As for wrath and envy [they] be the known children of pride, as rising of an high estimation of ourselves. But what should seem farther from pride than drunken gluttony? And yet shall ye find more that drink themselves sow drunk of pride to be called good fellows, than for lust of the drink self. So spreadeth this cursed root of pride his branches into all other kinds, besides his proper malice for his own part, not only in high mind of fortune, rule and authority, beauty, wit, strength, learning, or such other gifts of God, but also the false pride of hypocrites, that feign to have the virtues that they lack: and the perilous pride of them that for their few spotted virtues, not without the mixture of other mortal vices, take themselves for quick **1** saints on earth, proudly judging the lives of their even **2** Christians, disdaining other men's virtue, envying other men's praise, bearing implacable anger where they perceive themselves not accepted and set by after the worthiness of their own estimation. Which kind of spiritual pride, and thereupon following envy and wrath, is so much the more pestilent in that it carrieth with it a blindness almost incurable, save **3** God's great mercy. For the lecher knoweth he doth naught, **4** and hath remorse thereof; the glutton perceiveth his own fault, and sometimes thinketh it beastly; the slothful body misliketh his dulness, and thereby is moved to mend. But this kind of pride, that in his own opinion taketh himself for holy, is farthest from all recovery. For how can he mend his fault that taketh it for none, that weeneth all is well that he doth himself, and nothing that any man doth else, that covereth his purpose with the pretext of some holy purpose that he will never begin while he liveth, taketh his envy for an holy desire to get before his neighbour in virtue, and taketh his wrath and anger for an holy zeal of justice, and thus, while he proudly liketh his vices, he is out all the way to mend them; in so far forth that I surely think there be some who had in good faith made the best merchandise that ever they made in their lives for their own souls, if they had changed those spiritual vices of pride, wrath, and envy for the beastly carnal sins of gluttony, sloth and lechery. Not that these three were good, which be undoubtedly damnable, but for that like as God said in the Apocalypse unto the Church of Laodicea: "Thou art neither hot nor cold but lukewarm, I would thou were cold that thou mightst wax warm;" **5** signifying that if he were in open and manifest sins, he would have more occasion to call fervently for grace and help,—so, if these folk had these carnal sins, they could not be ignorant of their own faults. For, as Saint Paul saith, the fleshly sins be easy to perceive, **6** and so should they have occasion to call for grace and wax good, where now, by their pride taking themselves for good where they be naught, **7** they be far from all occasion of amendment, saving the knocking of our Lord, which always standeth at the door of man's heart and knocketh, Whom I pray God we may give ear unto and let Him in. And one of His good and gracious knocking is the putting us in remembrance of death, which remembrance, as I have said, let us see what stead it may stand us in against this cursed sin of pride. And surely against this last branch of pride, of such as repute themselves for holy, with the disdain of others, and an inward liking of all their spiritual vices, which they commend unto themselves under the cloak and shadow of some kind of virtue, most hard it is to take remedy by the remembrance of death, forasmuch as they reckon themselves thereby ready to go straight to heaven. But yet if they consider the labour and solicitation of our ghostly enemy, the devil, that shall at the time of their death be busy to destroy the merits and good works of all their life before, and that subtlest craft and most venomous dart and the most for them to avoid, shall be, under the colour of a faithful hope of heaven, as a thing more than due to their own holiness, to send them wretchedly to the fire of hell for their sinful and wilful blind presumption, I say, the remembrance and consideration of this perilous point and fearful jeopardy likely to fall on them at the time of their death, is a right effectual ointment long before in their life to wear away the web that covereth the eyes of their souls in such wise as they cannot with a sure sight look upon their own conscience.

As for all other kinds of pride, rising of beauty, strength, wit, or cunning, methinketh that the remembrance of death may right easily mend it, since that they be such things as shall shortly by death lose all their gloss, the owners wot ne'er how soon.

And as lightly may there, by the same consideration, be cured the pride of these foolish proud hypocrites, which are yet more fools than they that plainly follow the ways of the world and pleasure of their body. For they, though they go to the devil therefor, yet somewhat they take therefor. These mad hypocrites be so mad that where they sink in hell as deep as the others, yet in reward of all their pain taken in this world they be content to take the vain praise of the people, a blast of wind of their mouths, which yet, percase, praise them not but call them as they be. And if they do, yet themselves hear it not often. And sure they be that within short time death shall stop their ears and the clods cover all the mouths that praise them. Which, if they well and advisedly considered, they would, I ween, turn their appetites from the laud of silly **8** mortal men, and desire to deserve their thanks and commendation of God only, Whose praise can never die.

Now the high mind of proud fortune, rule, and authority, Lord God, how slight a thing it would seem to him that would often and deeply remember the death that shall shortly take away all this royalty, and his glory shall, as the Scripture saith, never walk with him into the grave **9** ; but he that overlooketh **10** every man, and no man may be so homely to come too near him, but thinketh that he doth much for them whom he vouchsafeth to take by the hand or beck upon, whom so many men dread and fear, so many wait upon,—he shall within a few years, and only God knoweth within how few days, when death arresteth him, have his dainty body turned into stinking carrion, be borne out of his princely palace, laid in the ground and there left alone, where every lewd lad will be bold to tread on his head. Would not, ween ye, the deep consideration of this sudden change so surely to come and so shortly to come, withdraw the wind that puffeth us up in pride upon the solemn sight of worldly worship? **11** If thou shouldst perceive that one were earnestly proud of the wearing of the gay golden gown, while the lorel **12** playeth the lord in a stage play, wouldst thou not laugh at his folly, considering that thou art very sure that when the play is done he shall go walk a knave in his old coat? Now thou thinkest thyself wise enough while thou art proud in thy player's garment, and forgettest that when thy play is done, thou shalt go forth as poor as he. Nor thou remembrest not that thy pageant may happen to be done as soon as his.

We shall leave the example of plays and players, which be too merry for this matter. I shall put thee a more earnest image of our condition, and that not a feigned similitude but a very true fashion and figure of our worshipful estate. Mark this well, for of this thing we be very sure, that old and young, man and woman, rich and poor, prince and page, all the while we live in this world we be but prisoners, and be within a sure prison, out of which there can no man escape.

And in worse case be we than those that be taken and imprisoned for theft. For they, albeit their heart heavily harkeneth after the sessions, yet have they some hope either to break prison the while, or to escape there by favour, or after condemnation some hope of pardon. But we stand all in other plight: we be very sure that we be already condemned to death, some one, some other, none of us can tell what death we be doomed to, but surely can we all tell that die we shall. And clearly know we that of this death we get no manner pardon. For the King by Whose high sentence we be condemned to die, would not of this death pardon His own Son. As for escaping, no man can look for. The prison is large and many prisoners in it, but the gaoler can lose none; he is so present in every place that we can creep into no corner out of his sight. For as holy David saith to this gaoler, "Whither shall I go from Thy spirit and whither shall I flee from Thy face?" **13** —as who saith, nowhither. There is no remedy, therefore, but as condemned folk and remediless in this prison of the earth we drive forth awhile, **14** some bound to a post, some wandering abroad, some in the dungeon, some in the upper ward, some building them bowers and making palaces in the prison, some weeping, some laughing, some labouring, some playing, some singing, some chiding, some fighting, no man, almost, remembering in what case he standeth, till that suddenly, nothing less looking for, young, old, poor and rich, merry and sad, prince, page, pope and poor soul priest, now one, now other, sometimes a great rabble at once, without order, without respect of age or of estate, all stripped stark naked and shifted out in a sheet, be put to death in divers wise in some corner of the same prison, and even there thrown in an hole, and either worms eat him under ground, or crows above. Now come forth, ye proud prisoner, for I wis ye be no better, look ye never so high, when ye build in the prison a palace for your blood, is it not a great royalty if it be well considered? Ye build the Tower of Babylon in a corner of the prison, and be very proud thereof; and sometime the gaoler beateth it down again with shame. Ye leave your lodging for your own blood; and the gaoler, when ye be dead, setteth a strange prisoner in your building, and thrusteth your blood into some other cabin. Ye be proud of the arms of your ancestors set up in the prison; and all your pride is because ye forget that it is a prison. For if ye took the matter aright, the place a prison, yourself a prisoner condemned to death, from which ye cannot escape, ye would reckon this gear as worshipful as if a gentleman thief, when he should go to Tyburn, would leave for a memorial the arms of his ancestors painted on a post in Newgate. Surely, I suppose that if we took not true figure for a fantasy, but reckoned it as it is indeed, the very express fashion and manner of all our estate, men would bear themselves not much higher in their hearts for any rule or authority that they bear in this world, which they may well perceive to be indeed no better but one prisoner bearing a rule among the remnant, as the tapster doth in the Marshalsea; or at the uttermost, one so put in trust with the gaoler that he is half an under-gaoler over his fellows, till the sheriff and the cart come for him.

Of Envy. Now let us see what help we may have of this medicine against the sickness of envy, which is undoubtedly both a sore torment and a very consumption. For surely envy is such a torment as all the tyrants of Sicily never devised a sorer. And it so drinketh up the moisture of the body and consumeth the good blood, so discoloureth the face, so defaceth the beauty, so disfigureth the visage, leaving it all bony, lean, pale, and wan, that a person well set awork with envy needeth none other image of death than his own face in a glass. This vice is not only devilish, but also very foolish. For albeit that envy, where it may over, **15** doth all the hurt it can, yet since the worst most commonly envieth the better, and the feebler the stronger, it happeth, for the more part, that as the fire of the burning hill of Etna burneth only itself, so doth the envious person fret, fume, and burn in his own heart, without ability or power to do the other hurt. And little marvel it is though envy be an ungracious graft **16** ; for it cometh of an ungracious stock. It is the first begotten daughter of pride, begotten in bastardy and incest by the devil, father of them both. For as soon as the devil had brought out his daughter, pride, without wife, of his own body, like as the venomous spider bringeth forth her cobweb, when this poisoned daughter of his had helped him out of heaven, at the first sight of Adam and Eve in paradise set in the way to such worship, **17** the devil anon took his own unhappy daughter to wife, and upon pride begat envy; by whose enticement he set upon our first parents in paradise, and by pride supplanted them, and there gave them so great a fall by their own folly that unto this day all their posterity go crooked thereof. And therefore ever since, envy goeth forth mourning at every man's welfare: more sorry of another man's wealth than glad of her own, of which she taketh no pleasure if other folk fare well with her. In so far forth that one Publius, a Roman, when he saw one Publius Mutius sad and heavy, whom he knew for an envious person, "Surely," quoth he, "either [he] hath a shrewd **18** turn himself, or some man else a good turn," noting that his envious nature was as sorry of another man's weal as of his own hurt.

I cannot here, albeit I nothing less intend than to meddle much with secular authors in this matter, yet can I not here hold my hand from the putting in remembrance of a certain fable of Aesop; it expresseth so properly the nature, the affection, and the reward of two capital vices, that is to wit, envy and covetousness. Aesop, therefore, as I think ye have heard, feigneth that one of the paynim gods came down into earth, and finding together in a place two men, the one envious, the other covetous, showed himself willing to give each of them a gift, but there should but one of them ask for them both; but look, whatsoever that one that should ask would ask for himself, the other should have the selfsame thing doubled. When this condition was offered, then began there some courtesy between the envious and covetous, whether of them should ask: for that would not the covetous be brought unto for nothing, because himself would have his fellow's request doubled. And when the envious man saw that, he would provide that his fellow should have little good of the doubling of his petition. And forthwith he required, for his part, that he might have one of his eyes put out. By reason of which request, the envious man lost one eye, and the covetous lost both. Lo, such is the wretched appetite of this cursed envy, ready to run into the fire, so he may draw his neighbour with him. Which envy is, as I have said, and as Saint Austin saith, the daughter of pride, in so far forth that, as this holy doctor saith: strangle the mother and thou destroyest the daughter. And therefore, look what manner consideration, in the remembrance of death, shall be medicinable against the pestilent swelling sore of pride, the selfsame considerations be the next **19** remedies against the venomous vice of envy. For whosoever envy another, it is for something whereof himself would be proud if he had it. Then, if such considerations of death as we have before spoken of in the repressing of pride should make thee set neither much by those things, nor much the more by thyself for them if thyself hadst them, it must needs follow that the selfsame considerations shall leave thee little cause to envy the selfsame things in any other man. For thou wouldst not, for shame, that men should think thee so mad to envy a poor soul for playing the lord one night in an interlude. And also couldst thou envy a perpetual sick man, a man that carrieth his death's wound with him, a man that is but a prisoner damned to death, a man that is in the cart already carrying forward? For all these things are, as I think, made meetly probable to thee before. It is also to be considered that since it is so that men commonly envy their betters, the remembrance of death should of reason be a great remedy thereof. For I suppose, if there were one right far above thee, yet thou wouldst not greatly envy his estate, if thou thoughtst that thou mightst be his match **20** the next week. And why shouldst thou then envy him now, while thou seest that death may make you both matches the next night, and shall undoubtedly within few years? If it so were that thou knewest a great Duke, **21** keeping so great estate and princely port in his house that thou, being a right mean man hadst in thine heart a great envy thereat, and specially at some special day in which he keepeth for the marriage of his child a great honourable court above other times; if thou being thereat, and at the sight of the royalty and honour shown him of all the country about resorting to him, while they kneel and crouch to him and at every word barehead begrace him, if thou shouldst suddenly be surely advertised, that for secret treason, lately detected to the King, he should undoubtedly be taken the morrow, his court all broken up, his goods seized, his wife put out, his children disinherited, himself cast into prison, brought forth and arraigned, the matter out of question, and he should be condemned, his coat armour reversed, his gilt spurs hewn off his heels, himself hanged, drawn, and quartered, how thinkest thou, by thy faith, amid thine envy shouldst thou not suddenly change into pity?

Surely so is it that if we considered everything aright and esteemed it after the very nature, not after men's false opinion, since we be certain that death shall take away all that we envy any man for, and we be uncertain how soon, and yet very sure that it shall not be long, we should never see cause to envy any man, but rather to pity every man, and those most that most hath to be envied for, since they be those that shortly shall most lose.

Of Wrath. Let us now somewhat see how this part of our medicine that is to wit, the remembrance of death, may cure us of the fierce ragious **22** fever of wrath. For wrath is undoubtedly another daughter of pride. For albeit that wrath sometimes riseth upon a wrong done us, as harm to our person, or loss in our goods, which is an occasion given us and it often sudden, by reason whereof the sin is somewhat less grievous, the rule of reason being letted for the while by the sudden brunt of the injury, not forethought upon but coming upon us unprovided,--yet shall ye find that in them which have so turned an evil custom into nature that they seem now naturally disposed to wrath and waywardness, the very root of that vice is pride, although their manner and behaviour be such beside, that folk would little ween it. For go they never so simply, look they never so lowly, yet shall ye see them at every light occasion testy. They cannot abide one merry word that toucheth them, they cannot bear in reasoning to be contraried, but they fret and fume if their opinion be not accepted and their invention be not magnified.

Whereof riseth this waywardness, but of a secret root of setting much by themselves, by which it goeth to their heart when they see any man less esteem them than they seem worthy to themselves?

Wilt thou also well perceive that the setting by ourselves is more than half the weight of our wrath? We shall prove it by them that would haply say nay. Take me one that reckoneth himself for worshipful, and look whether he shall not be much more wroth with one opprobrious and rebukeful word, as 'knave,' percase, or 'beggar' (in which is no great slander) spoken to his face by one that he reckoneth but his match or far under him, than with the selfsame word spoken to him by one that he knoweth and acknowledgeth for a great deal his better.

We see this point confirmed by all the laws made among men, which laws, forasmuch as the actions of trespass be given to revenge men not of the wrongs only done unto them in their bodies or their goods, but also of their contumelies, griefs, and despites, whereby they conceive any displeasure at heart, lest in lack of law to do it for them, they should in following their irous **23** affection, revenge themselves immoderately with their own hands,--the laws, I say, considereth, pondereth, and punisheth the trespasses done to every man, not only after the hurt that is done or loss that is taken, but an if it be such as the party grieved is like to be wroth withal, the punishment is aggrieved or diminished, made less or more, after the difference in degree of worship and reputation between the parties. And this is the provision of the laws almost in every country, and hath been afore Christ was born; by which it appeareth by a common consent that a man's own estimation, setting by himself, disdaining to take rebuke of one worse than himself, maketh his wrath the sorer.

For the assuaging whereof, the law contenteth him with the larger punishment of the offender.

And this so far forth that in Spain it is sorer taken, and sorer punished, if one give another a dry blow with his fist, than if he draw blood upon him with a sword. The cause is none other but the appeasing of his mind that is so stricken, forasmuch as commonly they take themselves for so very manly men that three strokes with a sword could not anger one of them so much as that it should appear that by a blow given him with a bare hand any man should so far reckon him for a boy that he would not vouchsafe to draw any weapon at him.

So that, as I said, it well appeareth by the common confession of the world, expressed and declared by their laws, that the point and readiness that men have to wax angry groweth of the secret pride by which we set overmuch by ourselves. And like as that kind of good anger that we call a good zeal riseth of that we set, as we should do, so much by our Lord God that we cannot be but wroth with them whom we see set so little by Him that they let not to break His high commandments,--so riseth of much setting by ourselves that affection of anger, by which we be moved against them with ire and disdain that displease us and show by their behaviour that they set less by us than our proud heart looketh for. By which though we mark it not, yet indeed we reckon ourselves worthy more reverence than we do God Himself only.
I doubt not but men will say nay; and I verily believe that they think nay; and the cause is, for that we perceive not of what root the branches of our sins spring. But will ye see it proved that it is so? Look whether we be not more angry with our servants for the breach of one commandment of our own than for the breach of God's all ten; and whether we be not more wroth with one contumelious or despiteful word spoken against ourselves than with many blasphemous words unreverently spoken of God. And could we, trow ye, be more moved with the diminishing of our own worship than God's, or look to have our own commandments better obeyed than God's, if we did not indeed set more by ourselves than Him?

And therefore this deadly sore of wrath, of which so much harm groweth, that maketh men unlike themselves, that maketh us like wood **24** wolves or furies of hell, that driveth us forth headlong upon sword points, that maketh us blindly run forth upon other men's destruction with our own ruin, is but a cursed branch rising and springing out of the secret root of pride.

And like as it is in physic a special thing necessary to know where and in what place of the body lieth the beginning, and, as it were, the fountain of the sore from which the matter is always ministered unto the place where it appeareth (for the fountain once stopped, the sore "shall soon heal of itself, the matter failing that fed it,--which continually resorting **25** from the fountain to the place, men may well daily purge and cleanse the sore, but they shall hardly heal it), likewise, I say, fareth it by the sore of the soul: if we perceive once the root and dig up that, we be very sure the branches be surely gone. But while the root remaineth, while we cut off the branches, we let **26** well the growing and keep it somewhat under, but fail they may not always to spring again. And therefore, since this ungracious branch of wrath springeth out of the cursed root of pride and setting much by ourselves, so secretly lurking in our heart that uneath **27** we can perceive it ourselves, let us pull up well the root, and surely the branch of wrath shall soon wither away. For taken once away the setting by ourselves, we shall not greatly dote upon that we set little by. So shall there of such humility, contempt and abjection of ourselves shortly follow in us high estimation, honour, and love of God, and every other creature in order for His sake, as they shall appear more or less lief **28** unto Him.

And since by the destruction of pride followeth, as I have said, the destruction of wrath, we shall apply to the repression of wrath the selfsame considerations in the remembrance of death that we before have shown to serve to the repression of pride. For who could be angry for the loss of goods, if he well remembered how little while he should keep them, how soon death might take them from him? Who could set so much by himself, to take to heart a lewd, rebukeful word spoken to his face, if he remembered himself to be as he is, a poor prisoner damned to death; or so very wroth as we be now with some bodily hurt done us upon some one part of the body, if we deeply remembered that we be, as we be indeed, already laid in the cart carrying towards execution.

And if the wretchedness of our own estate nothing moved us, which being such as it is, should if it were well pondered, make us little regard the causes of our wrath, considering that all the while we live we be but in dying, yet might the state of him that we be wroth withal, make us ashamed to be wroth. For who would not disdain to be wroth with a wretched prisoner, with him that is in the cart and in the way to hanging, with him that were a-dying? And of this would a man be the more ashamed, if he considered in how much peril and jeopardy of himself his own life and his own soul is, while he striveth, chideth and fighteth with another, and that ofttimes for how very **29** trifles. First, shame were it for men to be wroth like women, for fantasies and things of naught, if there were no worse therein. And now shall ye see men fall at variance for kissing of the pax, or going before in procession, or setting of their wives' pews in the church. Doubt ye whether this wrath be pride? I doubt not but wise men will agree that it is either foolish pride or proud folly.

How much is it now the more folly, if we consider that we be but going in pilgrimage and have here no dwelling-place, then, to chide and fight for such follies by the way. How much more shame and folly is it yet, when we be going together to our death, as we be indeed.

If we should see two men fighting together for very great things, yet would we reckon them both mad, if they left not off when they should see a ramping lion coming on them both, ready to devour them both. Now when we see surely that the death is coming on us all and shall undoubtedly within short space devour us all, and how soon we know not all, is it not now more than madness to be wroth and bear malice one to another, and for the more part for as very trifles, as children should fall at variance for cherry-stones, death coming, as I say, upon us to devour us all?

If these things and such others as they be very true, so they were well and deeply remembered, I little doubt but they would both abate the crooked branch of wrath and pull up from the bottom of the heart the cankered root of pride.

1 living.
2 fellow.
3 without.
4 evil.
5 Apoc. iii. 16.
6 Gal. v. 19.
7 Apoc. iii. 17.
8 simple, poor.
9 Ps. iv. 8.
10 looks down on.
11 honour, dignity.
12 worthless fellow, rogue.
13 Ps. cxxxix. 7.
14 drag along for a time.
15 prevail, have dominion.
16 shoot.

17 *honour.*
18 *ill, bad.*
19 *nearest, best.*
20 *equal.*
21 *See Introduction, p. 21.*
22 *raging.*
23 *angry.*
24 *mad.*
25 *returning*
26 *prevent.*
27 *scarcely.*
28 *dear*
29 *what mere.*

Part 3--Of Covetousness, Gluttony, and Sloth

Of Covetousness. Let us now somewhat see what this part of this medicine may do to the cure of covetousness, which is a sickness wherein men be very sore deceived. For it maketh folk to seem far of another sort than they be indeed. For covetous men seem humble, and yet be they very proud; they seem wise, and yet be they very foolish; they seem Christian, and yet have no trust in Christ; and, which most marvel is of all, they seem rich, and yet be very beggars, and have naught of their own.

As for pride of the possession of their goods, whoso be well acquainted with them shall well perceive it how heartily they rejoice where they dare speak and call their betters beggars, if money be not so rife **1** with them, because they regard it less and spend it more liberally.

Men ween them wise also, and so they do themselves, because they seem to have providence and be folk of foresight, and not to regard only the time present, but make provision for time to come. But then prove they more fools than they that live from hand to mouth. For they take at the leastwise some time of pleasure with their own, though they fare hard at another. But these covetous niggards, while they pass on with pain always the time present, and always spare all for their time to come, thus drive they forth wretchedly till all their time be past and none to come.

And then when they least look therefor, leave all that they have heaped to strangers that shall never can them thank. **2**

If ye will say there be no such fools, I might say that I have seen some such in my time. And if ye believe not me, I could find ye record. But to the intent ye shall not deny me but that there have been such fools of old, ye shall hear what Solomon said seven years ere I was born. "I have seen," saith he, "another plague under the sun, and it is common among men: a man unto whom God hath given riches, substance and honour, so that he wanteth nothing that his heart can desire, yet God hath not given him leave to eat of it or to enjoy it, but a stranger devoureth." **3** Of such sort of fools, also, speaketh the psalmist, thus: "A man disquieteth himself in vain, and heapeth up riches, and cannot tell for whom he gathereth them." **4** And in the forty-eighth Psalm, the prophet expresseth plainly the folly of such fools, "For," saith he, "both the rich and the poor shall die, and leave their riches unto strangers." **5** And surely where they seem Christian, they have none earthly trust in Christ; for they be ever afraid of lack in time to come, have they already never so much. And methinketh utterly on the other side, that albeit every man that hath children is bound by the law of God and of nature to provide for them till they be able at the least by the labour of their hands to provide for their bellies (for God and nature looketh not, as methinketh, much farther, nor thrust us not out of the paradise of pleasure to make us look and long to be lords in this wretched earth), yet, I say, meseemeth verily, that have we never so little, if we be not in spirit merry therewith, but live in puling and whimpering and heaviness of heart, to the discomfort of ourselves and them that are about us, for fear and dread of lack in time to come, it appeareth, I say, plainly, that speak we never so much of faith and of trust in Christ, we have in our hearts neither more belief in His holy words nor trust in His faithful promise than hath a Jew or a Turk.

Doth not holy Scripture say, "Cast thy thought into God and he shall nourish thee?" **6** Why takest thou thought now in thyself, and fearest to fail for food? Saith not our Saviour Himself, "Have no care for to-morrow," **7** and then furnisheth and enforceth His commandment by example, saying, "Look upon the birds in the air, they neither sow nor reap, nor gather to no barns, and your heavenly Father feedeth them. Are not ye far more excellent than they? Your Father in heaven knoweth that ye have need of all these things. Seek ye first for the kingdom of heaven and the justice of Him, and all these things shall be cast unto you beside"? **8** Whosoever he be that heareth this, and yet puleth and whimpereth for doubt and fear of lack in time coming, either he believeth not that Christ spoke these words (and then believeth he not the gospel) or else, if he believe that Christ spoke them and yet feareth lest He will not keep them, how believeth he Christ or trusteth in His promise? Thou wilt haply say that Christ would not for any trust of Him that thou shouldst not provide for to-morrow, but look to be fed by miracle. In this thou sayest true: and therefore He said not, 'Provide not for to-morrow, nor labour not for to-morrow.' In token whereof he sent the Jews double manna, weekly, the day before the sabbath day, to be provided for before the hand. But He said unto us, 'Have none anxiety nor care of mind for tomorrow.' For the mind would Christ have clean discharged of all earthly care, to the end that we should in heart only care and long for heaven. And therefore He said, long for first and chiefly the kingdom of heaven, and all these earthly things God shall cast unto us besides: showing thereby that by the hearty longing for heaven we shall have both twain.

And surely the things coming of the earth for the necessary sustenance of man, requireth rather the labour of the body than the care of the mind. But the getting of heaven requireth care, cure and ardent desire of the mind, much more than the labour of the body, saving that the busy desire of the mind can never suffer the body to be idle.

Thou wilt haply say, "What if I cannot labour, or have more small children to find than my labour of three days will suffice to feed for one day? Shall I not then care and take thought how they shall live tomorrow, or tell what other shift I shall find?" First shall I tell thee what shift thou shalt make in such case: and after shall I show thee, that if all shift fail thee, yet if thou be a faithful man, thou shalt take no thought. I say, if you lack, thou shalt labour to thy power by just and true business to get that thee and thine behoveth. If thy labour suffice not, thou shalt show thy state that thou hast little money and much charge, to some such men as have much money and little charge: and they be then bound of duty to supply of theirs that thee lacketh of thine. What if they will not? Then, I say, that yet oughtest thou not to take thought and care in heart or despair of God's promise for thy living: but to make thyself very sure, that either God will provide thee and thine meat by putting other men in the mind to relieve thee, or send thee meat by miracle (as He hath in desert wilderness sent some men their meat by a crow **9**), or else His pleasure is that thou and thine shall live no longer but die and depart by famine, as He will that some other die by sickness. In which case thou must willingly without grudge or care (which, care thou never so sore, cannot get thee a penny the more) conform thyself to His ordinance. For though He hath promised to provide us meat, yet hath He not promised it for longer time than Him liketh to let us live, to Whom we be all debtors of death. And therefore, though He sent Daniel meat enough by Habakkuk **10** the prophet into the lake among lions, yet sent He none at all to Lazarus, but let him die for famine at the rich glutton's gate. **11** There died he without grudge, without anxiety, with good will and glad hope, whereby he went into Abraham's bosom. Now if thou do the like, thou shalt go into a better bosom, into heaven, into the bosom of our Saviour Christ.

Now if the poor man, that naught hath, show himself to lack faith and to have no trust in Christ's words if he fear lack of finding, what faith hath then the covetous wretch, that hath enough for this day, for to-morrow, for this week, for the next, for this month, for the next, for this year, for the next, yea and peradventure for many years, yearly coming in, of lands, offices, or merchandise, or other ways, and yet is ever whining, complaining, mourning, for care and fear of lack many years hereafter for him or his children, as though God either would not, or were not able to keep His promise with us? And (which is the more madness) his care is all for the living of himself and his children, for some such time as neither himself nor his children shall haply live thereto. And so loseth he the commodity of all his whole life, with the fear of lack of living when he is dead. Now if he hap to have a great loss, in what heaviness falleth he then? For if he had ten thousand pounds, and thereof had eight thousand taken from him, he would weep and ween he were undone. And yet if he had never had but one, he would have thought himself a great rich man, where now for the loss of eight, twain can do him no pleasure. Whereof riseth this high folly, but of the blind covetous affection that he had to that he lost? If he had had it still, yet he would peradventure not have occupied it: **12** for this that is left is more than he will spend or haply shall need to spend. If ye would have spent it well, ye have no cause to be sorry of the loss, for God accepteth your good will. If ye would have kept it covetously or spent it naughtily, **13** ye have a cause to be glad and reckon that ye have won by the loss, in that the matter and occasion of your sin is by God's goodness graciously taken from you.

But ye will say that ye have now lost of your worship, and shall not be set by so much as ye were when ye were known for so rich. Ah well, I say, now ye come home, lo! Methought always that ye covetous niggards, how lowly soever ye looked, would if ye were well searched, prove yourself proud and high-hearted. For surely make they never so meek and humble countenance, they have much pride in the mind, and put their trust in their goods, making their goods their God. Which thing is the cause that our Saviour Christ said it were as hard for the rich man to come into heaven, as a great cable or a camel to go through a needle's eye. **14** For it is not sin to have riches, but to love riches.

"If riches come to you, set not your heart thereon," saith holy Scripture. **15** He that setteth not his heart thereon, nor casteth not his love thereon, reckoneth, as it is indeed, himself not the richer by them, nor those goods not his own, but delivered him by God to be faithfully disposed upon himself and others: and that of the disposition he must give the reckoning. And therefore, as he reckoneth himself never the richer, so is he never the prouder. But he that forgetteth his goods to be the goods of God, and of a disposer reckoneth himself an owner, he taketh himself for rich.

And because he reckoneth the riches his own, he casteth a love thereto, and so much is his love the less set unto God. For, as holy Scripture saith, "Where thy treasure is, there is thine heart"; **16** where if thou didst reckon the treasure not thine, but the treasure of God, delivered thee to dispose and bestow, thy treasure should be in earth and thy heart in heaven. But these covetous folk that set their hearts on their hoards, and be proud when they look on their heaps, they reckon themselves rich, and be indeed very wretched beggars: those, I mean, that be full christened in covetousness, that have all the properties belonging to the name, that is to wit, that be as loath to spend aught as they be glad to get all. For they not only part **17** nothing liberally with other folk, but also live wretchedly by sparing from themselves. And so they reckon themselves owners, and be indeed but the bare keepers of other men's goods. For since they find in their heart to spend nothing upon themselves, but keep all for their executors, they make it even now not their own while they use it not, but other men's, for whose use and behoof they keep it.

But now let us see, as I said before, how the remembrance of death may quicken men's eyes against this blind folly of covetousness. For surely it is an hard sore to cure: it is so mad that it is much work to make any good counsel sink into the heart. Wilt thou see it proved? Look upon the young man whom Christ Himself counselled to sell that he had and give it to poor folk, and come and follow Him. **18** He clawed his head and went his way heavily, because he was rich: whereas Saint Peter and other holy apostles at the first call left their nets, which was in effect all that they had, and followed Him. They had no great things whereupon they had set their hearts to hold them back. But an if their hearts had been sore set upon right small things, it would have been a great let. **19**

And no marvel though covetousness be hard to heal. For it is not easy to find a good time to give them counsel. As for the glutton, [he] is ready to hear of temperance, yea and preach also of fasting himself, when his belly is well filled,--the lecherous, after his foul pleasure past, may suffer to hear of continence, and abhorreth almost the other by himself. But the covetous man, because he never ceaseth to dote upon his goods, and is ever alike greedy thereupon, whoso giveth him advice to be liberal seemeth to preach to a glutton for fasting when his belly is empty and gapeth for good meat, or to a lusty lecher when his leman **20** is lately light in his lap. Scantly can death cure them when he cometh. I remember me of a thief once cast at Newgate, that cut a purse at the bar when he should be hanged on the morrow; and when he was asked why he did so, knowing that he should die so shortly, the desperate wretch said that it did his heart good to be lord of that purse one night yet. And in good faith, methinketh as much as we wonder at him, yet see we many that do much like, of whom we nothing wonder at all. I let pass old priests that sue for advowsons of younger priests' benefices. I let pass old men that hove and gape **21** to be executors to some that be younger than themselves: whose goods, if they would fall, they reckon would do them good to have in their keeping yet one year ere they die. But look if ye see not some wretch that scant can creep for age, his head hanging in his bosom, and his body crooked, walk pit-pat upon a pair of pattens with the staff in the one hand and the *pater noster* in the other hand, the one foot almost in the grave already, and yet never the more haste to part with anything, nor to restore that he hath evil gotten, but as greedy to get a groat by the beguiling of his neighbour as if he had of certainty seven score years to live.

The man that is purblind cannot see far from him,--and as to look on death, we be for the most part purblind all the meinie: **22** for we cannot see him till he come very near us. But these folk be not purblind but stark blind: for they cannot see him when he cometh so near that he putteth almost his finger in their eye. Sure the cause is for that they willingly wink, and list not to look at him. They be loath to remember death, loath to put this ointment on their eyes. This water is somewhat pricking and would make their eyes water, and therefore they refuse it. But surely, if they would use it, if they would as advisedly remember death as they unadvisedly forget him, they should soon see their folly and shake off their covetousness. For undoubtedly, if they would consider deeply how soon they may, yea, and how soon they must, lose all that they labour for, they would shortly cease their business, and would never be so mad, greedily to gather together that other men shall merrily soon after scatter abroad. If they thought how soon in what painful plight they shall lie a-dying, while their executors afore their face ransack up their sacks, they would, I ween, shortly empty their sacks themselves. And if they doubt how far that death is from them, let them hear what Christ saith in the gospel to the rich covetous gatherer that thought to make his barns and his warehouses larger to lay in the more, because he reckoned in himself to live and make merry many years: and it was said unto him: "Thou fool! This night shall they take thy soul from thee: and then these things that thou hast gathered, whose shall they be?" **23** And holy Saint Bernard saith that it may be said unto him farther; "thou that hast gathered them, whose shalt thou be?"

If we would well advise us upon this point and remember the painful peril of death that we shall so soon come to, and that of all that we gather we shall carry nothing with us, it would cause us to consider that this covetous gathering and niggardous keeping, with all the delight that we take in the beholding of our substance, is in all our life but a very gay golden dream, in which we dream that we have great riches, and in the sleep of this life we be glad and proud thereof. But when death shall once waken us, our gay golden dream shall vanish, and of all the treasure that we so merrily dreamed of, we shall not (as the holy prophet saith) find one penny left in our hands. **24** Which if we forgot not, but well and effectually remembered, we would in time cast covetousness out of our heads, and leaving little business for our executors after our death, not fail to dispose and distribute our substance with our own hands. If thou knewest very certainly, that after all thy goods gathered together, thou shouldst be suddenly robbed of all together, thou wouldst, I ween, have little joy to labour and toil for so much, but rather as thou shouldst happen to get it, so wouldst thou wisely bestow it there as need were and where thou mightst have thank therefor: and on them specially that were likely to help thee with theirs when thine were all gone. But it is so that thou art of nothing so sure as that death shall bereave thee of all that ever thou heapest, and leave thee scant a sheet. Which thing, if we did as well remember as we well know, we should not fail to labour less for that we shall so lose, and would put into poor men's purses our money to keep, that death, the cruel thief, should not find it about us, but they should relieve us therewith when the remnant were bereft us.

Of Gluttony. Now have we to consider how this part of our medicine, that is to wit, the remembrance of death, may be applied to the cure and help of gluttony, which is a beastly sickness and an old sore. For this was in the beginning joined with pride in our mother Eve: who besides the proud appetite that she had to be by knowledge made in manner a goddess, yet took she such delight also in the beholding of the apple, that she longed to feel the taste. And so entered death at the windows of our own eyes into the house of our heart, and there burned up all the goodly building that God had wrought therein. And surely so falleth it daily, that the eye is not only the cook and the tapster, to bring the ravenous appetite of delicate meat and drink into the belly (so far forth that men commonly say it were better fill his belly than his eye, and many men mind it not at all till they see the meat on the board), but the eye is also the bawd to bring the heart to the desire of the foul beastly pleasure beneath the belly. For when the eye immoderately delighteth in long looking of the beauteous face, with the white neck and round paps, and so forth as far as it findeth no let, the devil helpeth the heart to frame and form in the fantasy, by foul imaginations, all that ever the clothes cover. And that in such excellent fashion, as the mind is more kindled in the feigned figure of his own device than if it should haply be if the eye saw the body belly naked such as it is indeed. And therefore saith the holy prophet, "Turn away thine eyes from the beholding of vanities." **25** Now, as I began to say, since it is so that this old sore of gluttony was the vice and sin by which our forefathers, eating the forbidden fruit, fell from the felicity of paradise and from their immortality into death and into the misery of this wretched world, well ought we to hate and abhor it, although there should now no new harm grow thereof. But so is it now, that so much harm daily groweth thereof new, not to the soul only, but to the body also, that if we love either other, we see great cause to have it in hatred and abomination, though it had never done us hurt of old. For hard it is to say whether this vice be more pestilent to the body or to the soul: surely very pestilent to both. And as to the soul, no man doubteth how deadly it is. For since the body rebelleth always against the spirit, **26** what can be more venomous and mortal to the soul than gorbellied gluttony, which so pampereth the body, that the soul can have no rule thereof, but carrieth it forth like an headstrong horse, till he have cast his master in the mire. And if the corruptible body be (as the wise man saith) burdensome to the soul, **27** with what a burden chargeth he the soul that so pampereth his paunch that he is scant able to bear the burden of his own belly, though it were taken from that place and laid upon his back. If the body be to the soul a prison, how strait a prison maketh he the body that stuffeth it so full of rift-raff that the soul can have no room to stir itself, but as one were so set, hand and foot, in a strait stocks that he can neither stand up nor lie down,--so the soul is so stifled in such a stuffed body that it can nothing wield itself in doing of any good spiritual thing that appertaineth unto his part, but is, as it were, enclosed, not in a prison but in a grave, dead in manner already, for any good operation that the unwieldy body can suffer it to do.

And yet is gluttony to the soul not so pernicious and pestilent for the hurt it doth itself, as for the harm and destruction that is done by such other vices as commonly come thereon. For no man doubteth but sloth and lechery be the very daughters of gluttony. And then needs must it be a deadly enemy to the soul, that bringeth forth two such daughters, of which either one killeth the soul eternally,--I mean not the substance of the soul, but the wealth **28** and felicity of the soul, without which it were better never to have been born. What good can the great glutton do with his belly standing astrut like a taber, **29** and his noll toty **30** with drink, but balk **31** up his brews **32** in the midst of his matters, or lie down and sleep like a swine. And who doubteth but that the body delicately fed maketh, as the rumour saith, an unchaste bed. Men are wont to write a short riddle on the wall that D. C. hath no P. Read ye this riddle? I cannot: but I have heard say that it toucheth the readiness that woman hath to fleshly filth, if she fall in drunkenness. And if ye find one that can declare it, though it be no great authority, yet have I heard say that it is very true.

Of our glutton feasts followeth not only sloth and lechery, but often-times lewd and perilous talking, foolhardiness, backbiting, debate, variance, chiding, wrath, and fighting, with readiness to all manner mischief, running to ruin for lack of circumspection, which can never be without soberness. The holy Scripture rehearseth that in desert, the children of Israel, when they had sat down and well eaten and drunk, then rose they up and played the idolators whereof by the occasion of gluttony, the wrath of God fell upon them. **33** Holy Job, when his children fell to feasting, feared so greatly that the occasion of gluttony should in their feasts make them fall into foolish talking and blasphemy, that while they were about their feasts, he fell to prayer and sacrifice, that God might at his prayer send them grace so to make good cheer that they fell not in the vices usually coming of gluttony. **34** Now to the body what sin is so noyous, **35** what sin so shameful? Is it not a beastly thing to see a man that hath reason, so to rule himself that his feet may not bear him, but when he cometh out he weeneth that the sky would fall on his head, and there rolleth and reeleth till he fall down the kennel, **36** and there lie down till he be taken up and borne to bed as a corpse were borne in bier? And in good faith, in my mind much wrong is there done him that any man presumeth to take him up, and that he is not suffered to take his ease all night at his pleasure in the king's highway, that is free for every man.

Wonder it is that the world is so mad that we had liefer take sin with pain, than virtue with pleasure. For, as I said in the beginning and often shall I say, virtue bringeth his pleasure, and vice is not without pain. And yet speak I not of the world to come, but of the life present. If virtue were all painful, and vice all pleasant, yet since death shall shortly finish both the pain of the one and the pleasure of the other, great madness were it if we would not rather take a short pain for the winning of everlasting pleasure, than a short pleasure for the winning of everlasting pain. But now, if it be true, as it is indeed, that our sin is painful and our virtue pleasant, how much is it then a more madness to take sinful pain in this world, that shall win us eternal pain in hell, rather than pleasant virtue in this world, that shall win us eternal pleasure in heaven?

If thou ween that I teach thee wrong, when I say that in virtue is pleasure and in sin is pain, I might prove it by many plain texts of holy Scripture, as by the words of the psalmist, where he saith, "I have had as great pleasure in the way of Thy testimonies as in all manner of riches." *37* And Solomon saith of virtue thus, "Her ways are all full of pleasure, and her paths are peaceable." **38** And further he saith, "The way of the wicked is as it were hedged with thorns; but the way of the righteous is without stumbling." **39** "And we be wearied," shall the wretches say, "in the way of wickedness; we have walked in hard and cumbrous ways": and the wise man saith, "The way of the sinners is set or laid with stones, but in the end is hell darkness and pains." **40** But to tell us worldly wretches the words of holy Writ is but a dull proof. For our beastly taste favoureth not the sweetness of heavenly things. And as for experience, we can none get of the one part, that is to wit, the pleasure that is in virtue. The other part we cannot perceive for bitter, for the corruption of our custom whereby sour seemeth us sweet. But yet if we would consider our sin well, with the dependants thereupon, we should not fail to perceive the painful bitterness of our wallow **41** -sweet sin. For no man is so mad that will reckon that thing for pleasant that hath with little pleasure much pain. For so might we call a man of India white, because of his white teeth. Now if thou shouldst, for a little itch, claw thyself suddenly deep into the flesh, thou wouldst not call thy clawing pleasant, though it liked thee a little in the beginning. But so is it that for the little itching pleasure of sin, we claw ourselves suddenly to the hard bones, and win thereby, not a little pain, but an intolerable torment. Which thing I might prove beginning at pride in every kind of sin, saving that the digression would be over long; for the abridging whereof, let us consider it but in the selfsame sin that we have in hand.

The pleasure that the glutton hath in his viand can be no longer any very pleasure than while it is joined with hunger, that is to say, with pain. For the very pleasure of eating is but the diminishing of his pain in hungering. Now all that ever is eaten after, in which gluttony beginneth, is in effect pain altogether. And then the head acheth, and the stomach gnaweth, and the next meal is eaten without appetite, with gorge upon gorge and grief upon grief, till the gorbelly be compelled to cast up all again, and then fall to a rere **42** - supper.

If God would never punish gluttony, yet bringeth it punishment enough with itself: it disfigureth the face, discoloureth the skin, and disfashioneth the body; it maketh the skin tawny, the body fat and fobby, **43** the face drowsy, the nose dripping, the mouth spitting, the eyes bleared, the teeth rotten, the breath stinking, the hands trembling, the head hanging, and the feet tottering, and finally no part left in right course and frame. And besides the daily dulness and grief that the unwieldly body feeleth by the stuffing of his paunch so full, it bringeth in by leisure the dropsy, the colic, the stone, the strangury, the gout, the cramp, the palsy, the pox, the pestilence, and the apoplexy, diseases and sickness of such kind that either shortly destroy us, or else the worse is, keep us in such pain and torment that the longer we live the more wretched we be.

Howbeit, very long lasteth no man with the surfeits of gluttony. For undoubtedly nature, which is sustained with right little (as well appeared by the old fathers that so many years lived in desert with herbs only and roots) is very sore oppressed, and in manner overwhelmed, with the great weight and burden of much and divers viands, and so much laboureth to master the meat and to divide and sunderly **44** to send it into all parts of the body and there to turn it into the like and retain it, that she is by the force and great resistance of so much meat as she hath to work upon (of which every part laboureth to conserve and keep his own nature and kind such as it is) forwearied and overcome, and giveth it over, except it be helped by some outward aid. And this driveth us of necessity to have so much recourse to medicines, to pills, potions, plasters, glisters, and suppositaries: and yet all too little,--our gluttony is so great and therewith so diverse that, while one meat digesteth, another lieth and putrefieth. And ever we desire to have some help to keep the body in health. But when we be counselled to live temperately, and forbear our delicacies and our gluttony, that will we not hear of: but fain would we have some medicines, as purgations and vomits, to pull down and avoid that we cram in too much. And in this we fare (as the great moral philosopher Plutarch saith) like a lewd **45** master of a ship that goeth not about to see the ship tight and sure, but letteth by his lewdness his ship fall on a leak, and then careth not yet to stop the chinks, but set more men to the pump rather with much travail and great peril to draw it dry, than with little labour and great surety to keep it dry. "Thus fare we," saith Plutarch, "that through intemperate living drive ourselves in sickness, and botch us up with physic, where we might with sober diet and temperance have less need of and keep ourselves in health."

If we see men die some dear year by famine, we thereof make a great matter,--we fall to procession, we pray for plenty, and reckon the world at an end. But whereas yearly there dieth in good years great people of gluttony, thereof we take none heed at all, but rather impute the blame to the sickness whereof they die, than to the gluttony whereof the sickness cometh. And if there be a man slain of a stroke, there is, as reason is, much speech made thereof, the coroner sitteth, the quest **46** is charged, the verdict given, the felony found, the doer indicted, the process sued, the felon arraigned, and dieth for the deed. And yet if men would ensearch how many be slain with weapon, and how many eat and drink themselves to death, there should be found (as Solomon saith) more dead of the cup and the kitchen, than of the dent of sword **47** and thereof is no words made at all.

Now if a man willingly kill himself with a knife, the world wondereth thereupon, and, as well worthy is, he is indicted of his own death, his goods forfeited and his corpse cast out on a dunghill, his body never buried in Christian burial. These gluttons daily kill themselves with their own hands, and no man findeth fault, but carrieth his carrion corpse into the choir, and with much solemn service burieth the body boldly at the high altar, when they have all their life (as the apostle saith) made their belly their God, **48** and liked to know none other: abusing not only the name of Christian men, preferring their belly joy before all the joys of heaven, but also abusing the part and office of a natural man and reasonable creature. For whereas nature and reason showeth us that we should eat but for to live, these gluttons are so glutted in the beastly pleasure of their taste that they would not wish to live an it were not for to eat.

But surely wisdom were it for these gluttons well and effectually to consider that, as Saint Paul saith, "the meat for the belly and the belly to the meat: but God shall destroy both the meat and the belly." **49** Now should they remember and think upon the painful time of death, in which the hands shall not be able to feed the mouth, and the mouth that was wont to pour in by the pottle **50** and cram in the flesh by the handfuls, shall scant be able to take in three drops with a spoon, and yet spew it out again. Oft have they had a sick drunken head, and slept themselves sober; but then shall they feel a swimming and aching in their drunken head, when the dazing of death shall keep all sweet sleep out of their watery eyes. Oft have they fallen in the mire, and thence borne to bed; but now shall they fall in the bed, and from thence laid and left in the mire till Gabriel blow them up.

Whereas these considerations much ought to move any man, yet specially should it so much the more those gluttons, in how much that they may well wit that their manner of living must needs accelerate this dreadful day, and draw it shortly to them, albeit that by course of nature **51** it might seem many years off. Which thing if these intemperate would well and advisedly remember, I would ween verily, it would not fail to make them more moderate in their living, and utterly flee such outrageous riot and pestilent excess.

Of Sloth. Of the mortal sin of sloth men make a small matter. Sloth is a sin so common, and no notable act therein that is accounted for heinous and abominable in the estimation of the world, as is in theft, manslaughter, false forswearing, or treason, with any of which every man would be loath to be defamed, for the world perils that do depend thereupon,--that therefore of sloth there is no man ashamed, but we take it as for a laughing matter and a sport.

But surely since it is a great capital sin indeed, the less that we set thereby, the more perilous it is: for the less we go about to amend it. Now, to the intent that we do not deadly deceive ourself, it is necessary that we consider well the weight. Which if we do, we shall find it far greater than we would before have weened.

There are, ye wot well, two points requisite unto salvation, that is to wit, the declining or going aside from evil, and the doing of good. **52** Now whereas in the first part there are all the other six to be eschewed, that is to wit, pride, envy, wrath, gluttony, covetousness, and lechery, the other part, that is, the one half of our way to heaven, even sloth alone is able to destroy.
Sir Thomas More wrote no farther of this work.

1 plentiful.
2 can them thank=thank them.
3 Eccles. vi. 1-2.
4 Ps. xxxix. 6.
5 Ps. xlix. 10.
6 Ps. lv. 22.
7 Matt. vi. 34.
8 Matt. vi. 26-33; Luke xii. 24-31.
9 1 Kings xvii. 4.
10 Dan. xiv. 33 (Vulgate).
11 Luke xvi. 20. 12 put it to use. 13 wastefully.

14 *Matt. xix. 24; Mark x. 25; Luke xviii. 25.*
15 *Ps. lxii. 10.*
16 *Matt. vi. 21.*
17 *share.*
18 *Matt. xix. 21; Mark x. 21; Luke xviii. 22.*
19 *hindrance*
20 *mistress*
21 *wait greedily*
22 *company*
23 *Luke xii. 20.*
24 *Ps. xlix.*
25 *Ps. cxix. 37.*
26 *Gal. v. 17.*
27 *Wisdom ix. 15.*
28 *well-being*
29 *drum, tabour*
30 *dizzy*
31 *belch*
32 *broth*
33 *Ex. xxxii. 6.*
34 *Job i. 5.*
35 *hurtful*
36 *gutter*
37 *Ps. cxix. 14.*
38 *Prov. iii. 17.*
39 *Prov. xv. 19.*
40 *Ecclus. xxi. 11.*
41 *sickly, nauseatingly.*
42 *late*
43 *soft, flabby*
44 *in different directions*
45 *ignorant*
46 *jury*
47 *Ecclus. xxxvii. 34.*
48 *Phil. iii. 19.*
49 *1 Cor. vi. 13.*
50 *half-gallon*
51 *See p. 218 (101.D.1).*
52 *Ps. xxxiv.14; 1 Pet. iii. 11.*